Other books by Kay Wright


*The Divorce Concierge Is At your Service* (2015)

*Everything I Know About Relationships – I Learned from Barry Manilow* (2014)

*You Can Learn A Lot About Life & Love from a Barry Manilow Song* (2014)

*Journey to Joy – Inspiring Stories of Women Who Follow Their Hearts to Live in a Space of Joy* (2013) Contributing author.

*Pathways to Vibrant Health & Well-Being – Profound Stories of Physical, Emotional and Spiritual Healing to Encourage and Uplift You on Your Personal Journey* (2014) Contributing author.


Available through www.amazon.com

# Never Live Paycheck to Paycheck Again

## With Balloon Theory

# By Kay Wright

# Never Live Paycheck to Paycheck Again



Printed in the United States of America

First Printing, 2020

ISBN – 13: 9798643866893

Publisher: Kay Wright

Dedication

This book is dedicated to my two ex-husbands who showed me that I should never count on someone else's balloon to keep me afloat.

# Contents

# Contents

# Contents

# Introduction

The fact that you have selected this book makes me know that you are interested in making money, managing money and saving money.

If that sounds difficult – it isn't. I designed Balloon Theory to be a quick and easy way to gauge your financial health at a glance.

Perhaps you have been taught to believe that finances are too complicated or someone (a spouse maybe) made you feel that you just were not smart or savvy enough to manage your finances. That sort of thinking stops right now.

In the pages that follow, I will explain what Balloon Theory is and how it can be used to manage your home finances. Balloon Theory can also be used for debt reduction and asset building.

At its very core, Balloon Theory is a non-technical method to visualize and manage multiple revenue streams coming into your home or business. Balloon Theory can also help you visualize and reduce debt while increasing assets. There are no spreadsheets or complicated mathematical equations needed. You can do this. You can take charge of your life and future right now.

However, to get the full benefit from the information presented in the following pages, you will need to let go of current beliefs and tap into your inner child. So, gather up several sheets of construction paper of various colors, scissors, ribbon, crayons, paint and poster paper. You are going to create a personalized financial snapshot that reflects where you are now and where you want to be in the future. Let's go!

# The Changing Landscape

Many years ago, the one-income family was the norm – with dad going off to his job at the factory or office while mom stayed home to take care of the house and children. As more income was needed, the typical American family consisted of one full-time income plus one part-time income. Dad was still at his office or factory, but now mom made extra income, often by selling Avon or Tupperware, so that she could still be available to run the house and care for the children. Today, having one spouse staying home with the kids is not generally an option because it takes at least two full-time incomes to support a family.

In the past when more money was needed, a person would get an additional job or two (we called it moonlighting) that would augment their 9-5pm paycheck. The problem with that is, there are only 24 hours in a day and you need to sleep for 6-8 of those hours. When you had to physically be at a workplace, it limited how many hours you could possibly work, and therefore, how much money you could bring into your home.

The one income household could work when the expectation was that the wage earner would work for the same company their entire work life and then receive a pension from that company in retirement. Now, only a small fraction of the workforce can collect a pension, and even a smaller fraction of the current working population will stay with the same company. We are now responsible for saving for our retirements, while handling all the expenses of a home and family.

Today people are changing jobs more frequently because their company downsized, closed, or moved jobs out of the country. Manufacturing jobs are disappearing, and the only chance for advancement requires employees to move on to another employer. Today's graduates will change jobs approximately every 5-7 years during their working life. We now need to remain in the workforce longer because of these factors.

It sounds like the cards are stacked against us, doesn't it? How are we to manage as the economy puts more and more strain on us?

I believe the answer can be found in the pages that follow. But first, let's start with my story.

# My Story

I grew up in a 6-person household (2 parents and 4 children), who depended primarily on one income—my father's salary as a civil service postal worker. My mother worked sporadically over the years, in between having and raising kids. But it was my father's income that we depended on to feed, clothe and house us. There was no savings. We lived paycheck to paycheck.

Although we were not considered poor, there never seemed to be enough money to handle unexpected expenses, like when the stove conked out or the car needed a new transmission.

What did all this mean? If my father was laid off or fired from his job – the one job the entire family depended upon – we would have virtually no income, no real savings to tide us over until he could find work again, and no health insurance. We were basically a one balloon family.

So how did I handle finances when I was on my own and had graduated from college with massive student loan debt? I handled my money the only way I knew how – the way that was modeled to me by my parents – I lived paycheck to paycheck. I lived at home with my parents until I was able to get a job and save up enough for a down payment on a used car and handle the security deposit on an apartment. This took much longer than it could have if I had been taught to make savings a priority. But since my parents weren't savers, neither was I. I opened credit card accounts and used them to buy things I thought I needed, while paying only the minimum each month.

When I married at age 31, I discovered that my spouse had grown up with a very different financial model in his parent's household. He wasted no time on insisting that I adopt this plan.

Carrying credit card debt was not an option, so you can imagine his chagrin when he discovered that I had $3000 in credit card debt, in addition to my student loan debt. He set up a plan for us to pay of my credit card debt, but I had to vow that I would never carry credit card debt again. I could never again charge more than I could pay off the following month. It was tough at first, but when I realized that I saved all that interest the credit card company would have charged if I had a balance – I became a believer.

He set up a budget that did not allow for gifts to family for any occasion. Ouch! We each received an allowance that we could use for personal items, like going out to lunch or buying a new sweater (that one was for me). I received a whopping $25 per week.

Although our financial model was new to me, as our marriage progressed, we tended to follow a more traditional household financial model where he was the primary bread winner and I worked various marketing jobs to accommodate his career. My career was never able to get traction because we moved several times for his career, and in each location, I had to re-invent myself and start all over again. We were basically a two-balloon family -one large and the other small.

When my marriage ended, that large balloon was burst, and I came tumbling down to the ground without a large enough balloon to keep me afloat. If I had used Balloon Theory back then, I would have seen how precarious our financial situation was for me.

However, like Scarlett O'Hara declaring that she would never be hungry again, I vowed to never go back to living paycheck to paycheck. I used the tools I had learned in my marriage to create a stable financial plan for myself moving forward. Unencumbered by a spouse who kept telling me that I wasn't smart enough to handle financial investments, I had the freedom to jump in and make investment decisions.

After going through a very lengthy, litigious and expensive divorce, I designed a program that would show women how to avoid the mistakes I had made in my divorce, while saving a lot of money in the process.

At its very essence, divorce is a business transaction – deciding who gets what piece of the marital pie. The problem is that each party wants to keep the whole pie! Add in the emotional angst and anger, and you have the ingredients for a mass explosion that leaves multiple casualties in its wake.

I called my business WOMEN ON THE MEND. After all, weren't we all just trying to piece our lives back together? This is how I was going to support myself.

As I created the Divorce Concierge concept, I knew that I needed more than one way to bring money into my business. The technical term for this is Multiple Revenue Streams (MRS). I started doing research and made a list. I would counsel individuals, facilitate groups, be a speaker, write books and link to affiliate programs that offered products that were in alignment with my business. As time progressed, I envisioned my various revenue streams as a bunch of balloons-each representing a method of bringing in money.

Balloon Theory was a simple, quick, visual way to see how my business was progressing. As each method started to bring in money, I would change the color of its balloon. I also added additional balloons as I discovered more ways to bring in revenue. I could assess my business's health with a quick glance at my bunch. (I kept mine pinned to a bulletin board in my office.)

But my business was only a part of my bunch. I incorporated other income-producing assets into the mix that had nothing to do with my business.

No longer victimized by the negative messages I had received from my spouse, I took the lead, did my own research, designed a financial plan and invested resources into my bunch that would grow in value and provide me with monthly income.

I showed my clients that you can bounce back from a difficult life transition such as divorce by incorporating "Balloon Theory" into your life. You can structure your economic resources in a way that works for your unique lifestyle, schedule and parental responsibilities. With a strong bunch you can weather the various challenges you may face throughout your life.

So how do I handle my finances today? I no longer run WOMEN ON THE MEND, although I do still receive royalties for the books I wrote while I had that business.

I have incorporated a new business into my life that is in alignment with my current lifestyle and developed new non-business revenue streams. I also continue to benefit from resources I invested years ago. I carry no credit card debt – or any other debt, and I have automated my savings so that those assets continue to grow. Not bad for a woman who was told she wasn't smart enough to understand finances.

I no longer live paycheck to paycheck. And if you follow the principles included in this book and use Balloon Theory to master your finances, you will never live paycheck to paycheck again – ever.

# Balloon Theory

# What is Balloon Theory

Balloon Theory was designed to be a quick and easy way to gauge your financial health at a glance. At its very core, Balloon Theory is a non-technical method to visualize and manage multiple revenue streams coming into your home or business.

Those original circles I pinned onto my bulletin board in the shape of a bunch of balloons, were designed to encourage me to bring more than just one revenue stream into my home. I decided what balloons to add to my bunch. Because of this, I was able to create revenue streams that worked for my unique skill set and the overall situation I found myself in after my first divorce.

As I worked with Balloon Theory more and more, I came to realize that it can also help me visualize and reduce debt while increasing assets

You see, I was very familiar with the one-balloon financial plan. I had lived it in my twenties when I worked one 9-5pm job while accumulating debt and expenses. I lived in a mode of lack- and I made sure I stayed that way by buying things I didn't really need and increasing expenses at the same time.

I continued to spend hours each day commuting to a job that I liked, but that I knew had limited potential for advancement - professional or monetary. But I stayed because I had bills to pay and I did not have enough confidence in myself to believe that I could find another job closer to home.

Later, as a Career Counselor, I worked with countless folks who depended on one income to support themselves and their family. And when they lost that one paycheck due to down-sizing or other factors, their lives were thrown into chaos.

As I designed Balloon Theory for my own household, I was looking around for real-life examples. Other people must be doing this, right?

I found my examples right under my nose in the entertainment industry. To have a successful long-term career an actor needs to do more than act. They may start out as an actor but then add other ventures such as: product endorsement, voice over, books, personal appearances etc. Some have invested in restaurants, multi-media and liquor. George Clooney didn't make over $230 million dollars last year by acting. He made the bulk of it from the sale of his Casamigos Tequila Company.

I would lay odds that Oprah Winfrey has the biggest bunch of all. What doesn't this woman do? She is a talk show host, actor, producer, Weight Watchers owner/spokesperson and TV reporter for 60 Minutes. Oprah runs OWN TV, created HARPO Productions, created O Magazine and has a new product line of healthy foods called O Goodness.

Then there is the indomitable Joan Rivers. After the tragedy of her husband's death, Joan reinvented herself from stand-up comedienne into a talk show host, celebrity red carpet reporter, reality TV contestant (she won her season of Celebrity Apprentice), author, fashionista and jewelry designer. Her jewelry line would routinely sell out on her QVC appearances. Joan would do just about anything to stay relevant and make money. Good for you, Joan!

And what about financial guru Suze Orman? Suze started out as a waitress at a bakery (one income), and when she knew she had to make more money, became a stock broker (one bigger income). Since then, Suze has increased her bunch to include: TV host, author and motivational speaker. She has also designed various financial products that she sells through QVC and PBS.

Chip and Joanna Gaines from the HGTV show Fixer Upper, have increased their bunch from one balloon, Magnolia Homes Construction Company, into a multi-revenue bunch which now includes: Magnolia Home Furniture & Design, their TV show "Fixer Upper" on HGTV, Magnolia Market at The Silos-, Magnolia House Bed and Breakfast, The Magnolia Journal Magazine , The Magnolia Market & Silos Baking Company and The Magnolia Table restaurant. They have published two books, "The Magnolia Story" and "Capital Gaines". Target stores now carry their "Home & Hearth" line of home décor and furnishings.

Then there are celebrities with no real quantifiable talent, like Sharon Osborne and the Kardashians, who generate million-dollar revenues.

Celebrities really are masters at utilizing Balloon Theory. Here are some additional revenue streams that celebrities utilize:

Being paid for personal appearances

Participating in a Reality TV show such as Dancing with the Stars. You knew they got paid for that, right? Why do you think they are so happy when they escape elimination?

Acting in a TV show or movie

Producing a TV show or movie

Directing a TV show or movie

Voice-over for a TV show or movie

Writing Books – Celebrities love to talk about themselves or give advice.

Acting in commercials (often in overseas markets)

Receiving a percentage of the box office for movies that they have either starred in, produced or directed.

Receiving a percentage of movie rentals

Residuals from reruns of TV shows

Creating their own products

Infomercials

Product Endorsement-

Commercial/Ad voice-overs

Designing a furniture line

Creating and selling Fitness DVDs

Hawking their products on QVC-

Designing and endorsing a clothing line-

Creating a fragrance

Receiving revenue from concerts and music CDs

Participating or hosting TV game shows

Becoming a judge for a reality show

Becoming a host for a reality show

You think celebrities are different from us? You bet they are. But you can use the same system they use to create multiple revenue streams coming into your home.

Check out the Celebrity Balloon Theory Addendum at the end of this book for more examples of how the most successful celebrities have used this method to stay relevant, even relaunch careers, and continue to bring large sums of money into their bank accounts.

# How Balloon Theory Works

Balloon Theory allows you to decide how much and what type of revenue is coming into your household. You can structure your economic resources in a way that works for your unique situation, lifestyle, schedule, and parental responsibilities

You can toss away any preconceived ideas that financial management is difficult or only for the rich and start building your financial future right now.

Your balloon bunch will ultimately include revenue generating balloons, asset balloons and debt balloons so that you can assess your financial health at a glance. You will then be able to increase the buoyancy of your balloon bunch by doing one or more of the following:

Paying off debt

Increasing a current revenue stream

Adding a new revenue stream

Increasing a current asset

Adding a new asset

The reality is that nothing will change until you act. To assist you in taking the actions necessary to build a healthy bunch, included at the end of each section are worksheets you can use to answer important questions, take inventory, set goals and map out your action plan. What strategies will you use to add revenue streams to your household, pay down debt and ultimately increase your assets?

# Not All Money is the Same

To really understand Balloon Theory and reap the optimal rewards, it is imperative to understand that not all money is the same and that you do not have to go out and work for all revenue streams that come into your home or business. Your bunch should contain a combination of these four types of income.

## Active Taxable Income

What I call Active Taxable Income is the most common type of income we generate. It's the paycheck from your job working for an employer, who, by the way, has all the power to decide whether you continue to receive that paycheck or are unceremoniously given the heave-ho! It's the income documented on the W-2 earnings statement from traditional employment.

There is nothing wrong with Active Taxable Income. It should be a part of your household income stream. Notice I say a part, not the only, income stream. If you count on only Active Taxable Income, two things happen: 1. You limit how much income you can generate, and 2. You become entirely dependent on the whim of your employer.

## Active Non-Taxable Income

Active Non-Taxable income is revenue that you must physically do something to earn and is received as cash. Perhaps you help your neighbor clean out his garage or babysit or walk their dog and they insist on compensating you with some cash. Or you clean out your attic and have a yard sale

The other form of Active Non-Taxable Income is cash gratuities. There are many service industries, such as hospitality, where a cash gratuity is the norm. You leave a tip for excellent service at a restaurant and at your hairdresser. The folks in these jobs count on their tips to make a living wage. And since the bulk of these tips are received as cash, they tend to not be included on income tax forms. I had a friend who worked in the service industry and never claimed one penny of his gratuity income during his 30+ year career. Here are some examples of jobs where gratuities are an expected part of compensation:

Hairdresser/Barber

Delivery Person

Servers (waitress/busboy)

Valet (park car and bring back)

Bartender

Caddy

Hotel Room Cleaner

Charter Bus Driver

Taxi Driver

## Passive Taxable Income

Passive Taxable Income is revenue that you do not have to physically go out and do something to earn. Some examples are: dividends from brokerage accounts, interest from bank accounts, redemption of savings bonds, royalties from book sales, and monthly subscription/dues for business programs you may offer,

To generate Passive Taxable Income there is generally an initial activity that needs to be performed. For example, a brokerage account needs to be set up and financial research done before you can start to earn dividends; the book needs to be written and published before it can start to generate royalties; business programs need to be designed before you can offer them to your clients.

I know a business woman who created a video series on nutrition that she sells over and over to companies throughout the world. She has made thousands and thousands of dollars for a project she created years ago-once!

But after you have put in the initial investment of your time and skills, you can sit back and watch the money roll in. I will add, however, for maximum return, you should visit/manage these revenues on a regular basis.

## Passive Non-Taxable

Passive Non-Taxable revenue is the absolute best! You get to keep 100% and you don't have to do anything to get it! Here are 5 examples of passive-non-taxable revenues.

**Life Insurance Pay-Outs.** No tax due.

**Inheritance.** The tax is paid by the estate before you receive it.

**Gift Money.** Did you know that anyone can gift another person up to $15,000/year that is tax free for both parties? And you do not have to be a relative to receive this money. You can also receive up to $15,000 each from multiple people. Should you receive gift money from two people, that can be as much as $30,000 in your pocket – tax free.

**The Sale of Your Principle Residence** – There is no tax due on your home's increase in value up to $250,000 per individual, and up to $500,000 per couple.

**Municipal Bonds** -Most of the time, when you invest in bonds, you must pay federal, state and/or local tax on the yield you earn. However, when you earn money from municipal bonds, the proceeds are usually tax-free at the federal level and tax-free at the state level if you live in the same state in which the bonds were issued.

**Now let's start building your bunch!**

# Balloon Theory for Your Household

# Building Your Bunch

As Glinda, the Good Witch of the North, tells Dorothy in The Wizard of Oz, "It's always best to start at the beginning". So that is exactly what you need to do as your first step in building your bunch. Start with where you are now and then build a bunch that fits your needs and goals.

You will need to ask yourself the following questions, and maybe even more, to create your personal bunch.

How many sources of income do you currently have coming into your home? Are you a one-balloon household? Maybe two? And what type of income is coming in? Active? Passive? Taxable? Non-taxable?

Do you have enough money coming in to pay the bills and build college and retirement funds, while not depriving yourself of the activities and experiences that bring you joy?

Ask yourself, what would happen if one or more balloons disappear? Would you still have enough, or would your world be thrown into chaos?

After you have determined where you are currently, ask yourself these questions.

How much income do you need and where will it come from?

Do I need to add balloons and/or build in some passive income streams to add buoyancy to my bunch? If you can only list one or two primary revenue streams, then you will definitely need to do this. Don't feel bad. Most people fall into this category.

What are your unique revenue streams?

What additional revenue sources do you need to add?

Decide what kind of income you would like:

Active Taxable

Active Non-Taxable

Passive Taxable

Passive Non-Taxable

Recurring

Decide how much you want to come in from each source. Remember, it is best to include a combination of Active and Passive Income Sources

How much work do you want to do to get the revenue streams you desire?

Do you want to interact with people to get your revenues or work alone?

Do you want to create something once that will give you recurring income?


So, what does your bunch of balloons look like?

One lonely balloon or two or three...or have you designed a healthy bunch that generates revenues for you 24 hours a day?

# Managing Your Bunch

Once you have built your initial balloon bunch, it is imperative that you manage it to achieve optimal results. So, what do I mean when I say to manage your bunch? There are three actions you must take to manage your bunch: Review Regularly, Update Your Goals, and, most importantly, Do Not Take Your Bunch for Granted!

## Review Regularly

How often do you need to review your bunch? Review your bunch when you have paid off a debt or increased or added an asset or revenue.

I recommend reviewing your bunch every three months, with one of those reviews occurring at the beginning of each year. At this review, you should go over all your finances – income, assets and debt – and create your net worth statement and then set goals for the coming year.

What is the optimal number of balloons to have in your bunch? There really is no one magic number, although I would recommend that you have at last three good-sized revenue stream balloons. A combination of various sized active and passive revenue balloons creates more stability.

What does your bunch look like at this point?

Are your balloons creating the type and amount of income you desire?

What changes do you need to make?

How well have you done in accomplishing your goals?

## Update Your Goals

Your quarterly review will uncover the opportunity to update your goals. If everything is on track, you may not need to do this. However, it has been my experience that each time I review my bunch, I find additional ways to increase my financial health.

What steps do you need to take to update your goals? Do you need more revenue? There are basically two methods to increase your income. You can add balloons and/or increase the size of one or more existing balloons. If you have inactive balloons now is the time to activate them so that they generate revenue.

You may also want to adjust the ratio of active vs passive income. I don't know anyone who would not want to increase their passive income if they had the opportunity to do so.

Perhaps you started out with only active income. Don't be afraid to add new balloons as you think of additional ways to bring in cash. At the same time, don't hesitate to remove a balloon that is just not working for you. You also have the option of keeping it in the bunch but making it inactive.

Color coding your balloons is a quick, visual way to track your progress. Assign colors to various types of income, with inactive balloons reflecting a neutral tone. These inactive balloons will change color when they start to generate revenues. At a glance you can see your progress and set future goals to activate more balloons or increase the size of existing balloons.

## Don't Take Your Balloons for Granted

Just as any healthy relationship requires nurturing, your bunch needs your attention as well. You know what they say about assuming, right? Don't assume your bunch will just continue to bring in revenues. Economic conditions change. And that change can affect the buoyancy of your bunch.

Neglecting your bunch can result in balloons deflating, decreasing the revenues coming into your home. You can also miss opportunities to add balloons

Passive income can easily be taken for granted and forgotten. It may no longer be bringing in the revenue you need. Review it to make sure it is bringing the maximum amount that it can. Give it the attention it needs to work hard for you. So, YOU don't have to work hard!

# Balloon Theory Mistakes for Households

Depending on one revenue steam for the bulk or all your household income.

Only utilizing active taxable forms of revenue.

Not including your children, significant other, or other household members.

Not reviewing your revenue streams on a regular basis.

Not including smaller or non-traditional sources of income.

# Traditional Ways to Bring Revenue into Your Household

Wages from a full-time job.

Wages from a second job (we used to call this moonlighting).

Interest on savings and certificates of deposit.

Dividends from investments such as bond and equity dividend producing funds.

Alimony.

Child Support.

Pension.

Social Security.

# Creative Ways for Your Household to Generate Income

Combine generations into one household so that you have income from wages, investments, pensions and social security.

Become a Foster Parent.

Rent out a room. You can rent to students if you live near a college.

Turn your basement into an apartment and rent it out.

Refurbish old furniture and sell it at the local flea market.

Start a garden and set up a vegetable stand.

Pet sit for busy professionals or while owners are away on vacation.

Start a dog walking service.

House sit for owners while they are away.

Clean out your attic/garage and have a good old-fashioned yard sale. You will de-clutter at the same time.

Sell your clothes to consignment shops.

Give your opinion. You can earn points/money by doing on-line surveys such as: E-Rewards, Paid Viewpoint and Global Survey.

Be a Secret Shopper.

Drive. You can drive neighbors to appointments or drive for a car service such as Uber or Lyft.

Do odd jobs (Fiverr.com).

Offer handyman services.

Sell handmade items in etsy.com

Earn cash rebates for scanning your receipts using the Ibotta app.

Rent your driveway when there are special events such as a parade or concert in your area and local parking is limited.

Rent out your garage as extra storage or even for band practice.

Rent your stuff such as power tools, lawnmower and small cooking appliances.

# Household Income Worksheet and Action Item Plan

Take an inventory of your current income sources. How many sources do you have? Are they all active taxable income or do you currently have some passive income as well?

Active      Passive      Tax      Non-Tax

_______________________________________

_______________________________________

_______________________________________

_______________________________________

_______________________________________

_______________________________________

_______________________________________

_______________________________________

_______________________________________

If your income list is very limited or only contains active taxable income, part of your overall financial plan will be to create more income streams — both active and passive.

# Household Income Worksheet
## and Action Item Plan

Here are some questions to get you started

How much income do I need?

_______________________________________

_______________________________________

_______________________________________


What can I do to increase current income streams?

_______________________________________

_______________________________________

_______________________________________


What active and passive income streams can I add that fit into my unique abilities and lifestyle?

_______________________________________

_______________________________________

_______________________________________


Do I want to interact with people or work alone?

_______________________________________

_______________________________________

_______________________________________

# Household Income Worksheet
## and Action Item Plan

How much work do I want to do to get the revenue stream I desire?

_______________________________________

_______________________________________

_______________________________________

Am I in a position to create something (perhaps a product or book) once that will give me recurring or passive income?

_______________________________________

_______________________________________

_______________________________________

How much time do I want to spend in managing my income balloons?

_______________________________________

_______________________________________

_______________________________________

The one question you must NEVER as yourself is: Am I smart enough to successfully manage my finances. Because the answer is a resounding YES!

# Household Income Worksheet and Action Item Plan

What current income streams can you work on increasing?

_______________________________________

_______________________________________

_______________________________________

_______________________________________

_______________________________________

_______________________________________

_______________________________________

What new income streams can you add to your bunch?

_______________________________________

_______________________________________

_______________________________________

_______________________________________

_______________________________________

_______________________________________

_______________________________________

# Household Income Worksheet and Action Item Plan

Create balloons in different colors to represent each revenue source. For instance: green balloons for active taxable income, red for active non-taxable income, yellow for passive taxable income and blue for passive non-taxable income.

Any new income stream balloons should be represented by white balloons until they become active and start to bring in revenue.

Active          Passive          Tax          Non-Tax

________________

________________

________________

________________

________________

________________

________________

________________

________________

# Balloon Theory for Debt Reduction

# Building Your Debt Balloons

Our journey thus far has focused on bringing multiple revenue streams into your home/business, but that is just one piece of the puzzle.

To truly master your finances, you not only need cash coming in, you need to take control of any debt you may have. Fewer debts equals a brighter and stronger financial picture for you and your family.

Creating debt has become a way of life for us. Your first debt may have been from student loans needed to get you through college. While this is not the worst type of debt to have - you used these loans to obtain skills that made you more marketable in the business world - it is still a debt that needs to be paid off.

The next debt may be a car loan. After all, you need transportation to get where you need to go – hopefully a well-paying job in the profession for which you accumulated thousands of dollars in student loans.

Then come the credit cards. We are a society that seeks immediate gratification, and credit cards enable us to get things now that we really want but cannot afford. Before you know it, you are drowning in debt.

You can have multiple revenue streams coming into your home and additional assets, but if you have debt hanging over your head it negates the value of those assets and income.

Debt offsets your assets and lowers your net worth. Have you ever put together a personal net worth statement? I know, you thought net worth statements were complicated and only for the rich. Balloon Theory makes it easy.

# Not All Debt is the Same

Just as we discussed earlier that not all income is the same, not all debt is the same. For our purposes, let's divide credit into the following categories: light grey, medium grey and dark grey balloons.

**Light grey balloon** – You create this type of debt when you use a loan to purchase an asset that will increase in value such as a house, or to invest in an education which will increase your value in the job market. A loan for a rental property or even a boat that will generate revenue for you would also be considered light grey, or good debt. Your primary residence mortgage is considered a good debt because you can deduct the yearly interest and real estate taxes from your income taxes, plus, our homes generally increase in value. However, to get the maximum return you need to take care of the property and keep up with maintenance as well.

I am adding another type of loan to the good credit list, but it only works if you have self-discipline and have developed the habit of paying off debt in a timely fashion. This loan comes from retailers, such as furniture and appliance stores, who offer special financing that allows you to take between 6 and 18 months to pay off your balance without any interest. For this to stay in the good credit category, you MUST pay it off in the allotted time frame. If you don't, you will be charged interest dating all the way back to the time of purchase.

**Medium grey balloon** –You create this type of debt when you use a loan to purchase an asset that decreases in value such as an automobile, but it still serves a purpose and can be easily sold if it is maintained properly.

The down side to a car loan is that you are paying the loan based on the purchase price of the car and not the actual value, which is reduced the moment we drive off the dealership lot. The best scenario is to pay cash for your car, even if that means restricting your selection to older model vehicles.

**Dark grey balloon** – This category contains credit card debt, plain and simple. Credit cards left with ongoing balances are just a vicious cycle of interest charges and late fees. You think that blouse you got on sale was such a steal? The price of that item can increase exponentially if you are the kind of person who pays only the minimum monthly payment while maintaining an ongoing balance. If you must use credit cards, get in the habit of charging only what you can afford and pay off the entire balance each and every month.

Whether your debt balloons are light, medium or dark grey, they are all holding you down. Get rid of that weight and allow yourself, and your bunch, to fly!

# Benefits of Debt Reduction

The absolute best benefit of reducing/paying off your debt, is the feeling of calm and control you will have. There will be no more stress about pending bills, unpaid balances or even bill collectors knocking at your door.

You will also have more freedom to make choices regarding your money because now you will actually have money. When an emergency shows up, such as a medical diagnosis or household mishap, there is no need to stress out. You can handle this.

When you have an exemplary credit rating, say 750 and over, doors will open for you. You can get lower rates for future credit should you need it, such as mortgages and re-financing your home.

Just watch the car salesman roll out the red carpet the next time you visit his showroom! And when you can write a check for that new car, you are in a very good negotiation position. You can decide how much you will pay, not the salesperson.

Great credit scores also increase your chances of being selected for the job you desire. Companies are now checking applicant's credit scores as a gauge of their suitability. You see, they feel that employees with less debt and solid credit scores are a better risk – that they are less likely to steal from the company, whether it is in the form of cash, office supplies, less productivity or fudging on their timesheets. Employees with solid finances are less likely to call off from work due to transportation or child care issues.

I know what you are thinking. How can I develop a credit rating/score if I don't use credit? Although a debt-free life is the optimal goal, there are times when credit is the appropriate way to finance a step in your life such as education.

So, if you need student loans to get through school, you will develop a good credit rating by paying them off on time each month. The same goes for a car you may need to finance. By keeping up with the payments, you are building your score. Pay your rent and other bills such as utilities on time.

You can even obtain a credit card with a limited credit allowance that you pay off every month. The special financing from retailers that I mentioned previously, is also a way to develop a credit rating. If you practice responsible money habits on a regular basis, your credit score will reflect that.

# Managing Your Debt Balloons

Grey balloons are the debt that is weighing you down. Every time you pay off a debt you "pop" a debt balloon, which lightens the load and adds to the buoyancy of your bunch. So, your goal in managing debt balloons is to get rid of as many as possible, starting with the dark grey "bad" debt balloons.

Credit card debt first. This kind of debt (dark grey balloons) takes priority because it carries the highest interest rates. Make a list of all your credit card debt starting with the highest interest rate. Pay off the highest interest rate cards first.

You may prefer to pay off smaller credit card balances first if you want a quicker sense of accomplishment and to reduce the number of credit cards you are dealing with. Remember, however, that this is not the most efficient or cost-effective method.

Car loan comes next. You may have gotten a very low interest rate on your car loan, so you can work on paying it off after credit cards are handled.

Only then, your mortgage. Remember, this is considered "good" debt and consistent timely monthly payments help build your credit score.

Remember, credit is meant to be a tool, not a lasso around your neck or a balloon that weighs you down.

# Balloon Theory Mistakes for Debt Reduction

Not taking an accurate inventory of what you owe.

Not paying off debt in the correct order.

Paying off good debt.

Paying only the minimum payment on credit cards.

Continuing to use your credit cards irresponsibly.

Not paying off the most expensive debt first.

Not concentrating on paying off bad debt.

Not including debt reduction in your overall financial plan.

Not changing your behavior regarding spending & debt on a long-term basis.

Not creating a realistic budget that is based on what you can truly afford without going into debt.

# Debt Reduction Worksheet and Action Item Plan

Take an inventory of all debts you currently owe, their amounts, interest rate, and if they constitute a black, dark grey or light grey debt balloon. Create balloons in light, medium and dark grey to represent your debts.

**Debt**        **Amount**     **Rate**      **Color**

______________________________

______________________________

______________________________

______________________________

______________________________

______________________________

______________________________

______________________________

______________________________

______________________________

If you have a longer list of debt than this worksheet can fit, just get out another piece of paper and keep writing. This exercise can only work if you are completely honest.

# Debt Reduction Worksheet and Action Item Plan

Now. Make a list of your debt in the *order* that you plan to pay it off. Again, be honest here. The most cost-effective way to pay off debt is to handle the bad (dark grey balloon) debt first, but some people start with smaller debt, so they can feel a sense of accomplishment.

It is important to remember, that while you are paying off debt, you must still make at least the minimum payment to all your other debts.

| Debt | Amount | Rate | Color |
|------|--------|------|-------|
|      |        |      |       |

# Debt Reduction Worksheet and Action Item Plan

The third step is to figure out how you are going to pay off your debt. Where will the money come from? And what behaviors will you practice to make more money available and to ensure that you do not accumulate bad debt in the future.

The money to pay off my debt is coming from:

_______________________________

_______________________________

_______________________________

_______________________________

_______________________________

The new behaviors I will practice are:

_______________________________

_______________________________

_______________________________

_______________________________

Remember, all debt, especially bad debt, weighs you down. How many debt balloons will you "Pop!"

# Balloon Theory for Asset Building

# Building Your Asset Balloons

We've been focusing on methods to bring revenue into your home, but now we need to move on to building assets.

There is a saying that goes something like this, "It's not how much you make. It's how much you keep." You can have incredible amounts of money coming in from multiple streams, but a good part of the value is lost if you spend too much or build up large amounts of debt. We have seen this time and time again: the multi-million-dollar lottery winner who ends up broke, the overnight sensation who ends up declaring bankruptcy due to poor financial management, even our next-door neighbor who ends up foreclosing on his home because it was more important that he keep up with the Joneses, rather than live within his means.

First of all, let's determine what defines an asset. An asset is something that has value. It can either be sold or accessed to obtain monetary funds. You can take a loan against some assets, such as a home equity loan or personal loan against the value of your automobile.

Do you have any assets? I bet you do. So, let's identify assets you already have to determine where you are currently and what your plan needs to be moving forward.

Here is a list to get you started. Circle the assets you currently have. Add additional asset sources if necessary. Each asset will become a part of your asset balloon bunch.

Home

Automobile

401K

IRA

Savings Account

CDs

Rental property

After you have created an inventory of assets, the next step is to define them further.

## Liquid or Non-Liquid

Liquidity is determined by how easily you can access your assets. Some assets are very liquid, such as a savings account at your local bank, while others are less liquid, such as your IRA and 401K.

## Revenue Stream or Non-Revenue Stream

Does your asset also bring in a revenue stream to your home or business? You can count your home as a revenue generating asset if you rent out a room/garage or if you have an income property within it. i.e. apartment.

Your Asset Balloon Bunch should contain a mixture of liquid and non-liquid assets, revenue and non-revenue generating assets.

# Managing Your Asset Balloons

Do you have a mixture of asset sources in your bunch? Are they small balloons? Do they need to grow? Do you need to build more asset balloons?

Even small assets bring value to your bunch. Assets that start out small can grow over time as you add money to them and as they grow due to market conditions, such as a brokerage account, retirement accounts and your home.

My favorite type of asset is one that also serves as a revenue stream into your home. A brokerage account is as asset, but the dividends from it are also a revenue source. Remember passive income? Your home is an asset that should increase in value as the years go by, but it can also be a revenue source if you rent out an apartment. Some assets pretty much increase on their own such as real estate, stocks and bonds.

A good method to grow assets is to use automatic deposits into IRA/savings and set up automatic monthly purchases of stocks/treasury bonds. Here are three additional methods to grow your assets:

Max out the available 401K deduction from your paycheck.

Make maximum contributions to your IRA and ROTH IRA.

Set up a spousal IRA and contribute the maximum amount.

Remember, it is not enough to simply have an asset. Just like other parts of your bunch, an asset needs to be managed and maintained. Keep an eye on your brokerage accounts and play an active role in their management. Even with automated savings, you need to check on it at least twice a year to make sure it is still giving you the growth you desire. Tweak it if necessary.

And as for your material assets, such as your home(s) and automobiles(s), proper maintenance is essential.

# Balloon Theory Mistakes for Asset Building

Not automating your savings.

Not maxing out your 401K before-tax deduction in your paycheck.

Not contributing the maximum amount allowed to your IRA and ROTH IRA.

Not setting up and contributing to a spousal IRA, if your partner does not work outside the home.

Not understanding that even small assets are important.

Not generating income from your assets.

Giving up because you think that you don't have enough money available to make it worthwhile to save.

Allowing your fear to keep you from investing in the stock market, real estate, or even in yourself.

Giving up too soon because building assets does take time, discipline and a bit of courage as well.

Continuing to spend beyond your means.

# Asset Building Worksheet and Action Item Plan

Take an inventory of all your assets. Remember to include liquid and non-liquid assets, big and small assets and income-producing assets. An asset has value, whether it is in the form of cash or a rare stamp collection.

| Asset | Size | Liquid | Income |
| --- | --- | --- | --- |
| | | | |
| | | | |
| | | | |
| | | | |
| | | | |
| | | | |
| | | | |
| | | | |

If your asset list is currently very short or even non-existent, part of your overall financial plan will be a create more assets and increase the assets you may already have in your bunch.

# Asset Building Worksheet and Action Item Plan

Which current assets can you work on increasing?

____________________________________________

____________________________________________

____________________________________________

____________________________________________

____________________________________________

What new assets can you add to your bunch?

____________________________________________

____________________________________________

____________________________________________

____________________________________________

____________________________________________

____________________________________________

# Asset Building Worksheet and Action Item Plan

## Creating Your Asset Balloon Bunch

Make a balloon for each asset you currently have using different colors to represent:

Liquid Assets

Non-Liquid Assets

Income-Producing Assets

Non-Income Producing Assets

How many balloons are in your asset bunch? Are there enough to keep you afloat?

Now, create balloons in a new color that represent the additional assets you plan to add.

Do you have enough now? Remember, small balloons can get larger and your bunch will grow stronger with each asset you can activate.

# Balloon Theory for Expense Management

# Building Your Expense Bunch

Thus far, your journey to build your bunch has included revenues, assets and debt. Now you need to examine your expenses (where your money is going) in order to create financial health.

It doesn't matter how much or from how many sources you derive income. If your expenses are too high (putting out more than what is coming in) you cannot achieve financial health and stability.

Even if your expenses don't exceed your income, why should you pay more for something if you don't have to? Lowering your expenses also helps you increase your assets

Where are you spending your money? Whether it is in the fixed or flexible category, it pays to review each expenditure on a regular basis.

There are basically two types of expenses: Fixed (non-discretionary) and Flexible (discretionary).

Fixed expenses (non-discretionary) are something we must pay such as a mortgage on a home or rent for an apartment. Insurance is another. Utilities too. At its basic level, these expenses include our need for food, shelter and clothing. You may feel that there is nothing you can do about these expenses. They are what they are and cannot be changed.

Flexible expenses (discretionary) are items that we may want, or be used to having, but they are not absolutely essential. These expenses can include entertainment, leisure, travel, dining out, hobbies and more.

Now is the time to take an inventory of both fixed and flexible expenses to truly see how you are spending your money.

Create your current expense balloon bunch by creating balloons of different sizes and colors to represent fixed and flexible expenses.

Do you like what you see? Is your money really being utilized in ways that make your life more fulfilled? Or is your money just being thrown down the drain by paying too much for things you need that you could be getting for less? Or worse. Are you wasting money on meaningless stuff that adds no value to your life?

# Managing Your Expense Bunch

Now that you have identified where your money is going, let's take a look at ways to decrease both your fixed and flexible expenses.

### Fixed or Non-Discretionary Expenses

### Shelter

A mortgage can be re-financed at a lower rate.

You can move to a less expensive apartment.

You can get a roommate.

Real estate taxes can be appealed. There may be local discounts available for seniors and disabled veterans.

Homeowner's insurance can be bundled with auto insurance for a discount and deductibles can be increased to lower the cost.

A programmable thermostat allows you to adjust the heating/cooling in your home based on your schedule.

Use Energy Star appliances.

Keep your hot water heater at no higher than 120 degrees.

Turn the lights off.

Use energy efficient light bulbs.

## Food

Shop with a list.

Use coupons and shop weekly sales.

Limit the number of times you shop for food.

Eat meatless one day per week.

No more fast food or take-out food.

Make your own meals.

Limit the number of times you eat out.

## Clothes

Keep your clothes well-maintained.

Only purchase with sales and discounts.

Color-coordinate so that your clothes can serve multiple purposes and be used with other pieces to create unique outfits.

# Flexible or Discretionary Expenses

## Home

You need a telephone to communicate, but you don't necessarily need to purchase the newest model each time one is rolled out. And your kids do not need phones until they are old enough to care for them.

Bundle your cable/internet/phone for a better rate.

Purchase basic cable only. Do you really need all those channels that come at a premium price?

Limit the number of TVs in your home. Every member of the family does not need a separate TV. Plus, each TV/cable connection adds to your monthly bill.

## Entertainment

Get movies from your local library for free.

Attend free local concerts, plays, lectures, events.

Visit attractions that offer free or reduced admission days.

## Personal

Limit your use of beauty/nail salons.

Have a manicure/pedicure party at home with friends.

Color your own hair.

Limit your use of alcohol and cigarettes.

Cancel gym memberships.

Cancel newspaper and magazine subscriptions.

## Travel

Utilize points from credit cards to earn travel miles and free hotel rooms.

Use off-season specials to save.

USA Rail Pass - allows you to travel around the United States at one fixed price.

U.S. Park Pass – allows you access to 2,000 Federal Recreation sites across the country including our National Parks.

Visit Washington D.C – There are no admission fees to all the Smithsonian museums and the National Zoo.

# Expense Management and Action Item Plan

The first step is the determine what your expenses are currently. Start with your list of what you consider non-discretionary, or fixed, expenses and create balloons of various sizes to represent each expense.

**Expense**                    **Monthly Amount**

_______________________________________

_______________________________________

_______________________________________

_______________________________________

_______________________________________

_______________________________________

_______________________________________

_______________________________________

_______________________________________

_______________________________________

_______________________________________

_______________________________________

# Expense Management and Action Item Plan

Now make your list of what you consider discretionary, or flexible, expenses and create balloons of various sizes to represent each expense.

**Expense**                    **Monthly Amount**

_______________________________________

_______________________________________

_______________________________________

_______________________________________

_______________________________________

_______________________________________

_______________________________________

_______________________________________

_______________________________________

_______________________________________

_______________________________________

_______________________________________

_______________________________________

# Expense Management and Action Item Plan

If your expense balloons outweigh your revenue balloons, now is the time to go through each expense (fixed and flexible) to determine where cuts can be made. Remember, even fixed expenses can often be reduced.

**Expense     Action Needed to Reduce Amount**

___________________________________

___________________________________

___________________________________

___________________________________

___________________________________

___________________________________

___________________________________

___________________________________

___________________________________

___________________________________

___________________________________

___________________________________

# Expense Management and Action Item Plan

Now that you have set goals to reduce expenses or cut expenses outright, you can create a new set of balloons to represent your reduced expenses.

Remember, to be financially healthy, your revenue balloons must outweigh your expense bunch.

**Expense**                         **New Monthly Amount**

______________________________________

______________________________________

______________________________________

______________________________________

______________________________________

______________________________________

______________________________________

______________________________________

______________________________________

______________________________________

______________________________________

______________________________________

# Balloon Theory
# Success

# Your Bunch

If you have been following the action item worksheets throughout this book, you should now have designed a balloon bunch that reflects your current financial picture. This bunch needs to include income streams, debts, expenses and assets. Of course, you have the option to create a separate bunch for each category if you like.

If you opt to put everything into one large bunch it will include the buoyant income and assets balloons plus the heavy debt and expenses balloons that weigh it down.

Now take a good look. Do you like what you see? Do you have multiple income streams? Have you paid off/paid down your debt? Are your assets growing? Are your expenses less than your income?

Unless the answer is "yes" to the questions above, there is still work to do to create your optimal bunch. Remember, financial management doesn't have to be difficult or complicated. YOU create your bunch (or bunches). YOU set our goals. YOU decide how to create the financial health YOU deserve.

# Guidelines for Balloon Theory Success

Include active and passive income.

Include both small and larger revenue streams and assets.

Actively manage your discretionary and non-discretionary expenses.

Make a plan to pay down your debt. Get rid of or decrease the size and amount of debt balloons in your bunch. These balloons only weigh you down!

Never remove an income-producing balloon from your bunch until you have another one to take its place OR you have grown other balloons to a size where they are producing enough revenue to make up for the balloon you are removing.

Have a plan and actively manage your bunch.

Trust that you have the ability and the right to manage your money and achieve financial health.

Take control. You can do this.

# Final Thoughts

Do I practice what I preach? Absolutely! My bunch includes a mixture of active and passive income – some of which is taxable, some not. Not all my balloons are the same size. I have large, medium and small balloons. Don't negate the value of those small balloons. They help keep the bunch afloat. Plus, you can choose to grow them over time.

And I am proud to say that there are no debt balloons weighing me down.

Don't let anyone tell you that financial management is complicated. You can do this. The feeling of calm and control that comes with financial health is priceless!

Start popping those debt balloons, reducing expenses, adding revenue streams and building assets today! You are worth it.

Have fun!

# Celebrity Balloon Theory

Earlier in this book, I referred to celebrities using Balloon Theory. I have comprised a list below that includes examples of celebrities who use this theory to remain relevant in their chosen field and utilize skills in a unique way, while creating financial stability. It is also important to note that many celebrities on this list came from very normal, low- or moderate-income families.

## Tim Allen - Net Worth: $80 million

Actor on TV shows

Voice of Buzz Lightyear in Toy Story movie trilogy ("To Infinity and Beyond!")

Movies (The Santa Clause)

Spokesman/voiceover for Chevrolet and Campbells

Author

## Valerie Bertinelli - Net Worth: $25 Million

TV actress (One Day at a Time/Hot in Cleveland)

Spokesperson- Jenny Craig

Author – autobiography

Host of a cooking show on the Food Network

<u>**Ty Burrell**</u> **- Net Worth: $26 Million**

TV Actor (Modern Family)

Voice-Over for films

TV Ads

<u>**George Clooney**</u> **- Net Worth: $500 Million**

TV actor

Movie actor/director/screenwriter

Businessman

<u>**Cindy Crawford**</u> **- Net Worth: $100 Million**

Model

Furniture designer

Spokesperson – natural beauty skin care line infomercial

<u>**Jane Fonda**</u> **- Net Worth: $120 Million**

TV and movie actress

Fitness guru – books and DVDs

Author – autobiography

### Steve Harvey - Net Worth: $160 Million

Live comedy shows

Toured with The Kings of Comedy

Radio Show

Books (on relationships no less!)

Host of game show (Family Feud)

Host of TV Talk show

Host of Little Big Shots

### Kathy Ireland - Net Worth: $350 Million

Model

Fitness guru – DVDs

Branding expert

Furniture line

Clothing line

Kathy Ireland Worldwide marketing firm

**Heidi Klum - Net Worth: $90 Million**

Fashion Model/Victoria's Secret Model

Project Runway Host and Producer

Line of children's clothing (which she has tied into Project Runway)

Women's lingerie line

Judge on "America's Got Talent"

**Jennifer Lopez - Net Worth: $400 Million**

Sings and dances on tour while selling CDs and other tour paraphernalia

Acts in movies and TV

Judge on "American Idol" I believe she received $12 million for that

Judge on "The World of Dance"

Commercial endorsements for L'Oréal

Perfume

Clothing line at Kohl's

**Sharon Osbourne - Net Worth: $220 Million**

Managed her husband Ozzie Osbourne's band – Black Sabbath

"The Osbournes" reality tv show

Celebrity Apprentice

The Talk

America's Got Talent judge

The X-Factor (British) judge

**Rachel Ray - Net Worth: $60 Million**

TV cooking show host

Cookbook author

Line of household products (kitchen dinnerware/pots & pans/linens)

Pet food

Co-Host of Celebrity Cooking Show

**Arnold Schwarzenegger - Net Worth: $300 Million**

Body builder

Actor

Politician

**Ryan Seacrest - Net Worth: $410 Million**

Host of "American Idol" and now co-host of "Live! With Kelly & Ryan"

Host of daily radio show

"E" entertainment host

Producer (name tv shows he produces (Keeping Up with the Kardashians)

Reported for NBC from the Olympics in London/Rio

**Brooke Shields - Net Worth: $25 Million**

Model

Actress

Spokesperson (Lay Z Boy furniture)

**Suzanne Sommers - Net Worth: $100 Million**

TV actor

 Las Vegas entertainer

Author

Product endorsement (remember thigh master?)

Make-up and facial care

Health spokesperson

**Sophia Vergara - Net Worth: $160 Million**

TV Actor

Clothing Line

Commercials

**Betty White - Net Worth: $75 Million**

Game show celebrity (Password/Match Game)

TV actor (MTM Show/Golden Girls/Hot in Cleveland)

Animal Rights Activist

Whew!!

Celebrities continue to generate income for their estates from multiple revenue streams even after their death. The estates of Michael Jackson, Marilyn Monroe and Elvis Presley continue to generate millions each year.

# Celebrity Balloon Theory Worksheet

Now it is your turn. Make a list of your favorite actors, TV personalities, authors, chefs etc. Under each name make a list of all the ways they generate revenue

Name: _______________________

_______________________________
_______________________________
_______________________________
_______________________________

Name: _______________________

_______________________________
_______________________________
_______________________________
_______________________________

Name: _______________________

_______________________________
_______________________________
_______________________________
_______________________________

# Celebrity Balloon Theory Worksheet

Now it is your turn. Make a list of your favorite actors, TV personalities, authors, chefs etc. Under each name make a list of all the ways they generate revenue

Name: _______________________

_______________________________________

_______________________________________

_______________________________________

_______________________________________

Name: _______________________

_______________________________________

_______________________________________

_______________________________________

_______________________________________

Name: _______________________

_______________________________________

_______________________________________

_______________________________________

_______________________________________

# Celebrity Balloon Theory Worksheet

Now it is your turn. Make a list of your favorite actors, TV personalities, authors, chefs etc. Under each name make a list of all the ways they generate revenue

Name: _______________________

_______________________________________

_______________________________________

_______________________________________

_______________________________________

Name: _______________________

_______________________________________

_______________________________________

_______________________________________

_______________________________________

Name: _______________________

_______________________________________

_______________________________________

_______________________________________

_______________________________________

# Celebrity Balloon Theory Worksheet

Now it is your turn. Make a list of your favorite actors, TV personalities, authors, chefs etc. Under each name make a list of all the ways they generate revenue

Name: _______________________

_______________________________________

_______________________________________

_______________________________________

_______________________________________

Name: _______________________

_______________________________________

_______________________________________

_______________________________________

_______________________________________

Name: _______________________

_______________________________________

_______________________________________

_______________________________________

_______________________________________

# ABOUT THE AUTHOR

Kay Wright is an author, speaker and coach who was determined to never live paycheck to paycheck again when an unexpected divorce left her on her own for the first time in over twenty years. Kay designed Balloon Theory as a visual way to keep track of her finances. By using Balloon Theory, anyone can create financial health to keep themselves afloat through life's ups and downs.

Kay is also the author of " Don't Go Broke During a Divorce". Available on www.amazon.com